Seeker's
Guide to the
Spiritual
Wilderness

Thirty Life-Lessons from the
Appalachian Trail

_____

Craig and Suzy Miles

(LNT: Please do not leave this book in any shelter)

(handwritten: y ... in our path & on His Trail! Craig)

Seeker's Guide to the Spiritual Wilderness
Copyright © 2010 by Craig and Suzy Miles

Unless otherwise indicated, all Scripture quotations are taken from the Holy Bible, *New Living Translation*, copyright 1996, 2004. Used by permission of Tyndale House Publishers, Inc., Wheaton, Illinois 60189. All rights reserved.

Scripture taken from the Holy Bible, *New International Version*. Copyright © 1973, 1978, 1984 Biblica. Used by permission of Zondervan. All rights reserved.

Scripture taken from *The Message*. Copyright 1993, 1994, 1995, 1996, 2000, 2001, 2002. Used by permission of NavPress Publishing Group.

Cover: Joel Leachman in Vermont
Photo © 2009 Cortney Leachman

ISBN: 1449570755
EAN-13: 9781449570750

Printed in the United States of America

To God:
the Great Guide
in the spiritual wilderness
and
the Thorough Teacher
of life's lessons

To our children:
may you lean on and learn from
your Spiritual Father
each day

Table of Contents

Preface

When we set out to hike the Appalachian Trail as "Clay" and "Branch," we knew that God had many lessons in store for us. Knowing that we desired to seek God in each element of our hike, we carefully chose our trail names.

Craig took on the name "Clay" after Isaiah 45:9 because he desires to be moldable in God's hand. Suzy took on the name "Branch" after John 15:5 because she wants to remember that she can do nothing apart from God.

We left behind our real names, all our belongings, and our friends and family on a cold March day as we began a life-changing journey. Every day, God taught us lesson upon lesson that we continue to refer to back home in the "real" world.

It is our prayer that God will use these daily readings to connect you to the Vine so that He can mold you into the person He wants you to be (John 10:10).

Introduction

The trail can be thought of as a metaphor for our lives. There are struggles, ups, downs, roots, rocks, blue skies, and storms that each of us face as time passes by.

Each of us carries burdens. The burdens are sometimes physical and can feel like a heavy backpack. They are sometimes emotional burdens like divorce or death of a loved one. Sometimes the burdens are spiritual. The spiritual burden can be the heaviest of all.

In order to find out who we are and who we need to be, we all need a wilderness experience. The wilderness is where we are tested. The wilderness is also where there is solace. The silence of the woods is where we hear God.

By reading the Miles' experiences on the trail in one hand and meditating on the Bible in the other hand, this book is intended to lessen your burdens and to be a light to your spiritual path towards God's Holy Mountain (Psalm 99:9; Ezekiel 20:40).

Day 1
Mouse on My Arm!

As Paul gathered an armful of sticks and was laying them on the fire, a poisonous snake, driven out by the heat, bit him on the hand...But Paul shook off the snake into the fire and was unharmed. (Acts 28:3, 5)

It was another turbulent night on the trail. Because it was both stormy and early in the thru-hiking season, the shelter was packed well beyond capacity. Everyone in the shelter slept shoulder-to-shoulder, one person slept on top of a covered picnic table, and others even slept in the mud underneath the mouse-infested shelter.

As the last rays of diffused daylight were doused by the rain, everyone dove into their sleeping bags to escape the coming coldness and darkness that would soon invade the cramped shelter. Not wanting to disturb anyone, Clay rushed to put his headlamp on his arm, hang his backpack, and leap in his cold sleeping bag.

No one was stirring this night but Clay could not sleep a wink. One man on the right side of the shelter was rhythmically snoring...HONK...and a man on the other side of the shelter was answering him...SHEW! Like a long, six-set tennis match, Clay listened for hours as the two men served and volleyed hypnotic snores to each other all night long. Honk! Shew! Honk! Shew! Honk! Shew! Honk! Shew...!

Around midnight he found himself drifting in and out of sleep. That is, until he felt something scurry across his hand. With eyes now wide open he thought, "The mice are active tonight and no one hung their food!" Not feeling any threat, he shrugged it off and tried to gather more moments of sleep.

About an hour later, he felt the sensation on his hand again. Then he felt it again...and again! Clay sprung up like a jack in the box. As if trying to jettison a live grenade, he grabbed it tightly and tried to toss it out of the shelter. It must have latched on to his shirt with its gnarly little teeth because when Clay tried to throw it, it kept hitting his arm.

Now alarmed, he shouted to the darkness, "There's a mouse on my arm and it won't let go! There's a mouse on me!" Frantically, Clay grabbed the creature one last time as to throw him. Something was different this time. With his arm cocked and poised to throw, Clay's fingers noticed that the creature had no hair! In fact, it felt sort of smooth and round. It was his head lamp!

Clay was shocked but, because of the darkness, no one knew that it was not a mouse. So, he sheepishly announced to the awakened shelter, "I think the mouse is gone now."

Soon, the snoring resumed its call and answer as Clay cowered in his sleeping bag. But this time, it was a little warmer from the red glow of his embarrassed face.

Today's Scripture: Hebrews 12:1-2

Today's Action: Today, when I am faced with a poisonous enemy or even when I am my own worst enemy, in faith, I will depend on God and shake off what is hindering me (Ephesians 4:22-24; Colossians 3:9-10).

Today's Thoughts:

_____

_____

_____

_____

Day 2
Full Armor Fights No-see-ums

A final word: Be strong in the Lord and in his mighty power. Put on all of God's armor so that you will be able to stand firm against all strategies of the devil. For we are not fighting against flesh-and-blood enemies, but against evil rulers and authorities of the unseen world, against mighty powers in this dark world, and against evil spirits in the heavenly places. (Ephesians 6:10-12)

It was "Africa hot" that day—all day. Our hiking crew was ready for a short respite at Matt's Creek shelter. We had earned it. We had already hiked ten miles by noon that day—a "10 by 12" in hiker lingo. PB and J's were on the lunch menu and would serve to fuel the second half of the day. The big goopy mess looked delectable.

We were not the only ones having lunch today. A swarm of no-see-ums (a.k.a. the biting midge), nearly invisible flying insects that love to bite their unsuspecting victims, were dining on us! The camp was full of hikers dancing in pain while trying to eat their lunch.

After just one or two bites from the buggers, Clay hurriedly donned his blistering hot rain gear. Beads of sweat began dripping from the sleeves and even from the little eating hole he'd made by cinching down the rain hood. He may have looked silly, but better to be silly than to be bitten. As the other hikers took notice of how funny Clay looked, infectious laughter began to spread around the camp. Ironically, within just a few minutes the dancing hikers were all forced to cut their break short and abandon camp due to the no-see-ums. Clay, in his rain gear, was the only one left enjoying his sandwich through his little mouth hole.

Today's Scripture: Ephesians 6:10-18

Today's Action: Today I may be bitten by little temptations swarming around. So, I will put on the full armor of God (Ephesians 6:10-18). Even though the full armor of God may not be comfortable, it will certainly protect me from invisible predators (1 Corinthians 10:12-13).

Today's Thoughts:

_____

_____

_____

_____

_____

_____

_____

_____

_____

_____

_____

_____

Day 3
Trail Names

A good name is more desirable than riches; to be esteemed is better than silver or gold. (Proverbs 22:1, NIV)

On the trail, people often assume another identity. A person may be called "Fred" at home, but his name may be "Featherfoot" on the trail. There seem to be a few categories of trail names.

In one category of trail name, the name is supposed to describe an *outstanding characteristic* or quality of that person. An example of this type of trail name is "Two Cents Worth." She was given this name because she has an opinion about everything.

Some trail names do not describe the person's primary characteristics but they may have a particular *funny story* attached to them. In this category, the best name that we've heard was "Cold Feet." He obtained this name because he left his fiancé' in order to hike the trail. "Backdraft" received his name for other reasons.

Another type is one that simply sounds funny but the *trail name has no real significance* to the characteristic of the person. Some of our favorite names in this category are "Stinkerbell," "Super Trooper," and "Hippie Longwalking."

To us, *the best names seem to have significance.* In the Bible, often times when people came into a meaningful relationship with God, their names were changed to signify some outstanding characteristic about them. For instance, Abram means "exalted father" (Genesis 11:27) but Abram's name was changed by God to "Abraham" after God made a covenant with him (Genesis 15). Abraham means "father of great number" for this was God's promise to Abraham. Jacob is another example. Jacob's name means "heel catcher," "trickster," or "supplanter." This was because he was holding his twin brother's heel when they were born (Genesis 25:26) and, later in their lives, Jacob tricked their father for his brother's birthright (Genesis 27). After Jacob wrestled with the angel of the Lord, God changed his name to "Israel" (Genesis 32:28). Israel means "he fights or persists with God."

Today's Scripture: Exodus 3:13-14

Today's Action: What name best describes me? Starting today I will seek to have a good name in the sight of God and man (Proverbs 3:3-4). The name of the wicked will rot (Proverbs 10:7b). So, I will strive to make my name better than a fine perfume (Ecclesiastes 7:1).

Today's Thoughts:

_____

_____

_____

_____

_____

_____

_____

_____

_____

_____

Day 4
Daily Divine Appointments

We can make our own plans but the Lord determines our steps. (Proverbs 16:9)

Circumstances often dictate our day. We make plans, we prepare to execute those plans, and then a monkey wrench is thrown in the gears! On the trail and on the trail of life, we call these thwarted plans "daily divine appointments" because it is in these moments that we expect to see God at work.

Many times on the trail God made His will known to us by allowing us to speed up, slow down, or by halting us—usually through injury. One week, we were allowed to hike four, twenty-mile days to catch some friends of ours that we needed to see. Another time, Branch had a peculiar hip injury for five days. The time needed for healing allowed us to be encouraged by a group of college students we commissioned and it afforded Clay the time to lead his own father to know the Lord. Another injury Clay incurred allowed us to write this devotional. Indeed, God sets up circumstances such that we can be used by Him. We just need to be aware.

Hiking out of Elk Park, North Carolina, we had planned on hiking about eighteen miles to Moreland Gap shelter in Tennessee. Towards the end of the hiking day, a terrible storm blew in. It felt like the hosts of Heaven were shooting us with painful ice-pellet BB guns from the sky. Hiking fast, but still many miles from the shelter, Clay spotted a flat area and he wanted to set up camp to get out of the line of fire. However, Branch rightly suggested that we keep moving--despite the pelting. After all, the hail would shred our paper-thin tent, she rightly reasoned.

The hail made our steps swift towards the shelter. When we arrived, we met people who had *shortened* their hiking day due to the hail. No one was leaving. The hail had halted all of us.

As we surveyed the shelter to see who was there, Clay hung his head low when he saw that three from the party crowd were with us tonight. "Three partiers and two prayer warriors here...there is no way that we'll have any meaningful conversations tonight," he calculated. But God had other plans.

Held captive by the hail, we all sat in close quarters cooking in the shelter. One partier happened to be a doctor and, in the course of conversation, he had made several relativistic claims concerning medical ethics. The other two nodded with him in agreement. Unbeknownst to the doctor, for years now, we have studied the relation between God and ethics and, on this day, Clay had just listened to and memorized the structured arguments from a talk about that very topic on his MP3. How fitting!

As the night progressed, the weather was cold, but the friendly conversation warmed the shelter. As we reasoned together, they quickly became convinced that at least one universal objective moral value exists. By the next morning, two of them wanted to know more. Indeed, God had sent the hail that day to change everyone's plan in order to match His own.

Today's Scripture: Proverbs 16:9

Today's Action: Just as Philip was led by the Spirit to talk to the Ethiopian eunuch (Acts 8:26-40), just as persecuted Christians were scattered to proclaim God's good news (Acts 11:19), just as Paul's plans drastically changed due to a storm (Acts 27), and just as Jonah was forced to go back to Nineveh when he was swallowed by a whale (Jonah 1-2), today, when my plans are postponed, I will seek to recognize God's daily divine appointment.

Today's Thoughts:

Day 5
Snow Day

He went on board the boat to escape the flood—he and his wife and his sons and their wives. The only people who survived were Noah and those with him in the boat. (Genesis 7:7, 23c)

The sky was crystal blue as we hiked during the warm April day. Some hikers were heading into town upon hearing the weather report.

Our hippie friend said, "When the weatherman says 'flurries,' I ain't got no worries. If he says 'snowin,' then it's to town I'm goin'."

"That's right!" said Branch. "I'm in short sleeves. 'Accurate weatherman' is an oxymoron."

That night, while the wind whistled warning, the man in the moon was wearing a halo and the stars winked at us as if to assure us that everything was going to be alright. With stomachs full, we slipped into our feather-filled sleeping bags and dreamed deeply.

Before daylight, the flurries lightly tapped our tent to let us know they had arrived and they gently lulled us back to sleep again. But at first light we woke up to the once taut tent touching our faces. The snow had arrived!

Beating the snow off of the sagging tent, we sat up. Cold assaulted our bodies as we struggled to get out of our sleeping bags and put on all of the layers of clothing that we possessed. Digging our way out of the tent revealed a white lunar-looking landscape. It was both beautiful and terrifying. Stepping out of the tent, we sank into snow up to our knees. For a few minutes we played like children skipping school on a snowy day. Then reality set in. We were in trouble. We tried to cook but neither our fuel nor our lighter would ignite. We were in trouble. We tried to bite into our energy bars but they were frozen solid. We were in trouble!

Our feet blindly felt their way down the trail. Unable to see through the thick layer of snow, we tripped over root and rock alike. The white blaze that normally marked the trail was cleverly camouflaged by the snow-draped trees. Eventually, we made it to a road with virgin snow. No one had traveled on it since the snow began. With steep mountains on either side of us, we had two choices. Either climb another 1,600 vertical feet into deeper snow, sleep in our tent and try to make fire, or walk 15 miles into town to a warm hotel. Since they were calling for more "flurries" today, we started a long downhill day towards town.

With snow continuing to fall in large clumps, mileage came slowly. Tired from yet another misstep, Branch buried her face in her hands, sat in the snow, and prayed. Just when all seemed hopeless, we heard the unmistakable sound of a truck busting through the snow behind us. It was a local pastor who had canceled church services! He graciously allowed us into his SUV, braving more treacherous road to take us into town. His sacrifice spoke sermons to us. Like Noah, he graciously took us into the warmth of his "ark" to safety.

Today's Scripture: Psalm 91:14-16

Today's Action: Today I will keep a clean heart so that when I am in a desperate situation, I can call on the Lord with confidence to rescue me (Daniel 3:8-30).

Today's Thoughts:

_____

_____

_____

Day 6
Twisted Ankle

Next Paul and Silas traveled through the area of Phrygia and Galatia, because the Holy Spirit had prevented them from preaching the word in the province of Asia at that time. Then coming to the borders of Mysia, they headed north for the province of Bithynia, but again the Spirit of Jesus did not allow them to go there. (Acts 16:6-7)

It was our second year of long-distance hiking and we asked God to guide our paths as we set out. After our first night on this trip, we woke up at first light, peeked out of our tent, and surveyed the picnic table. We saw an animated middle-aged man weaving a story. It was our friend from last year named Struttin' Bird!

The previous year he did not really stand out in physical appearance but he shined in his personality. However, something had changed about his physical appearance this year. He seemed so skinny, disheveled, and tired. How could this be? He soon recognized us and we started catching up with each other.

He explained that the year he had hiked northbound with us he had finished all 2,175 miles of the trail. But he didn't get enough. So, he walked another 2,175 miles southbound during the winter. That's called a "yo-yo" in trail talk. He still didn't get enough. So, he said that he was going to walk it again—6,525 miles in a year and a half! That's called a "yo-yo-yo!"

Speaking past his sweet-smelling pipe, he had the entire camp laughing as he shared stories about a scary grouse and an annoying mouse. Having Struttin' Bird back in our path seemed to be God-ordained. It was only day two and God already seemed to be placing engaging people in our path with whom to chat with.

"God is so *fate*ful!" we rejoiced.

Leaving the shelter, we leisurely hit the trail. The three of us must have looked like some sort of "trail train." Struttin' Bird was up front puffing smoke like an engine, Clay was in the middle immediately behind him shoveling coal to his ego so he'd regale us with more stories, and Branch was in the caboose red-faced from side-splitting laughter. It must have been all of the belly laughs that caused Clay to pay less attention to the trail because *all it took was one second to turn his ankle.*

Now, Clay had turned his ankle tens of times before but this was different. In the past, he'd yell and hop around. This time all he could say was, "Oh no." *In the end, he had split a tendon and had to wear a protective cast for three months.*

As we were forced from the trail we asked, "Why would God allow this? Weren't we doing His work?" God had other plans. He was able to use us even more mightily off the trail than He may have on the trail. Off the trail, we provided chaplain care to two serious situations, we oversaw fifteen churches wanting to help hikers, we were able to assist two trail missionary friends for several weeks at a time, and we were able to write this devotional. God is great at opening and shutting doors.

Today's Scripture: Acts 16:6-10

Today's Action: Today I will seek to be in the center of God's perfect will (Romans 12:2). When I am faced with the choice between two decisions today, like Paul in Acts 16, I will ask God to help me to discern between a good decision and a better decision. I will accept when He changes my plans and I will work heartily where He has placed me (Acts 18:5-6).

Today's Thoughts:

_____

_____

_____

_____

_____

_____

_____

_____

_____

_____

_____

Day 7
Pure Water...Poo Water

Your boasting about this is terrible. Don't you realize that this sin is like a little yeast that spreads through the whole batch of dough? (I Corinthians 5:6)

The summer sun slow-cooked us like frogs in a kettle. If you try to breathe the air from a hot hair dryer, you'll feel what we felt. We were parched and needed relief. The guidebook to the trail said that there was a reliable water source just a mile ahead. With that promise, we slaked our thirst by finishing off our water supply.

Our swift steps to the stream were suddenly made slow when we saw a sign.

Just behind us, a pride of superhikers also walked up to the watering hole. The group of lightweight backpackers was known for never purifying water. Being such quick hikers, they must not have seen the sign. Like lions lapping up liquid, they stuck their bottles into the silted water and they started to drink deeply.

As if seeing someone about to drink poison, Clay jumped up and shouted, "Wait! Don't drink the water!"

A hiker with long dreadlocks said, "No worries, man. We won't get sick. If the water is movin', we're groovin'." His hippie brother joined in the chorus, "Yeah. If it's flowin', we're goin'."

Wide-eyed and without a word, Branch pointed them to a sign above the stream that changed everyone's day. The sign said, "Do not drink water...cow died upstream." Reading the words of warning, their faces dropped as did their bottles.

With a puckish grin Clay said, "It will take *a lot* of filtering to help to get the dead cow flavor out of the water!"

From that day forward the superhiker's lightweight backpacks were just a little heavier—by the weight of a water filter.

Today's Scripture: I Corinthians 5:1-13

Today's Action: A little drop of poison in a glass of pure water taints the whole glass. In the same way, a little bit of impurity in my life taints my fellowship with God and others. Christ can purify all of my impurities (1 John 1:7). Today I will pay attention to God's written statutes (Psalm 119), to the law He has written on my heart (Ezekiel 36:26), and to the Holy Spirit (John 16:7-14) so that I may be pure. Similar to breathing out, I will confess impurity as it occurs, and I will "breathe in" God's purifying forgiveness.

Today's Thoughts:

_____

_____

_____

_____

_____

_____

_____

_____

_____

Day 8
Bad Berry

Watch your life and doctrine closely. Persevere in them, because if you do, you will save both yourself and your hearers. (I Timothy 4:16, NIV)

Branch's purple teeth shone brightly behind a huge grin as she dived into a massive bush of blackberries. She did a jig as purple fingers dropped yet another handful of God's bounty into her now purple-stained skirt. Hobble berries, blackberries, and even apples were on the menu. We weren't making great time as we hiked through the Vermont A.T. The sun heated everything around us and the fragrance of sweet berries continuously distracted us from our mileage goals.

As we grazed through the forest, it was obvious which berries we should not eat. For example, the white Dolls Eyes berries are poisonous. They are bright white with an iris-looking dot in the center of them. They are not appealing to the sight. As you approach this bush, it is as if hundreds of eyes are staring at you! The very sight of them kills the

29

appetite. Who wants to eat something that looks like doll's eyes? Everyone shies away from them.

As Branch continued to graze, a particularly luscious berry caught her eye. Stopping to examine it, she considered its edibility. "Well, it looks like a blueberry and grows right next to the hobble berries. I'll bet that it's alright," she reasoned to Clay as he stopped beside her. So, she promptly picked the berry in question and placed it on her tongue. As soon as her mouth closed over the berry, her face contorted in a kind of confused revulsion. Her eyes watered and she immediately spit out the vile berry. She quickly rinsed her mouth hoping to wash away any lingering trace of the nasty taste.

Gasping for air she uttered, "It foamed in my mouth!"

Examining the rest of the berries of that type around us, she made sure not to make that mistake again. It was hard to believe that the glistening berry that looked so juicy and satisfying may have been poisonous. It tasted like whipped cream on an onion!

That afternoon we easily made our mileage goals as Branch most definitely slowed down her berry picking. Not wanting to relive the sensation of the bad berry, she was more careful to examine the berries before biting into them.

Today's Scripture: I Timothy 4:16

Today's Action: Today I will be a fruit inspector. *I will inspect fruit of life and fruit of doctrine.* If I am producing rotten fruit (Galatians 5:19-21), I will connect to the true Vine (John 15:5). By abiding in the Vine, I will naturally produce the fruit of the Spirit (Galatians 5:22-23). I will also check my teaching and the teaching of others against the word of God (I Thessalonians 5:21).

Today's Thoughts:

_____

_____

_____

_____

_____

_____

Day 9
Storms

Then Jesus got into the boat and started across the lake with his disciples. Suddenly, a terrible storm came up, with waves breaking into the boat. But Jesus was sleeping. The disciples went to him and woke him up, shouting, "Lord, save us! We're going to drown!" And Jesus answered, "Why are you afraid? You have so little faith!" Then he stood up and rebuked the wind and waves, and suddenly all was calm. (Matthew 8:23-27)

There was little sleep one night during our trek through the northern end of the Great Smoky Mountain National Park. All night long, clamorous lightning and huge hunks of hail hammered the plastic roof of the cramped and cold shelter.

Hiking on the ridge line the next morning, we could see for miles despite the uniform gray blanket covering the ominous sky. In the distance, danger lurked. A giant mass of dark clouds was displaying the same strobe lights as the night before. The storm we named 'Godzilla' looked to be an hour away.

Knowing that we were six miles from the next shelter, we picked up our pace. We needed to hike fast so that Godzilla would not overtake us.

With about two miles to go, the lumbering giant hit us with all his fury. Day became like night as rain, hail, thunder, and lightning engulfed us at once. Our metal trekking poles felt more like lightning rods while flashes of light and booming sounds surrounded us.

On the exposed ridgeline, there was nowhere to hide. Fearing for our lives at times during the drenching dash, we borrowed courage from God as we pleaded for protection.

The last two miles of blurred trail seemed like a violent, eternal car wash. At long last we made it to the shelter. As we dripped our way through the door, one hiker caught our eye. It was our atheist friend. He looked shell shocked. Tightening his grip on his sleeping bag, he recounted to us what had happened to him. He said that a bolt of lightning struck right next to him. Like a scared soldier under heavy fire, he took cover in a rocky trench and prayed until another hiker came to his aid and walked with him to the shelter. We understood. We were shaken too. So, sitting around the shelter fireplace, we swapped stories and shared with him some of the courage that helped to calm the storm in our heart that day.

Today's Scriptures: Psalm 107:23-31; 139:7; Philippians 4:6-7; Hebrews 13:5

Today's Action: When the chaotic storms of life hit me, how will I react? Most people crouch, run, or hide. While these are appropriate actions during dangerous times, I will call upon the Lord in faith to calm the physical storm as well as the storm in my heart and my head (2 Samuel 22).

Today's Thoughts:

_____

_____

_____

_____

_____

_____

Day 10
Mountaintop Perspective

The Lord looks down from Heaven and sees the whole human race. (Psalm 33:13)

We had been hiking with Mountain Crab for three days and he was not happy about the trail or life. He croaked about crawling up Sassafras Mountain, he growled about the grade of Ramrock Mountain, and he squawked about the steepness of Big Cedar Mountain. Indeed, these are tough climbs.

"Why did the trail club make the trail go up that mountain? They could have gone an easier way, couldn't they?" he groused.

In the course of conversation, he also revealed that he was unhappy about the way God ran the world. "If God is all powerful, all knowing, and all good, then why is there evil?" he asked.

At mile thirty, we took a day off from hiking at the on-trail hostel. Branch asked Mountain Crab, "Would you like to see why the trail club chose to route the trail the way they did? It's the best view of the trail and it's only a thirty-minute walk." Although there was a remnant of snow still spotting the ground and the mileage didn't count, Crab was keen on the idea.

Hiking on an old Civilian Conservation Corps trail near the A.T., up the mountain we went. "Don't turn around." Clay said. "We have a surprise for you." Getting towards the top, the snow increased. Finally, it was time to turn around. With the leaves off of the trees, we could see mountain after mountain spread out like the elevation profile on a topographic map. We were looking at twenty-five miles of A.T. in one glance.

From our keen vantage point, to the left we could see Black Mountain—near mile twenty. Crab had not complained about that mountain. This is because *the trail club mercifully chose to place the trail to the side of the mountain instead of over the 3,600' top.* So, no hiker notices Black Mountain.

A little to the right of Black Mountain, we could see Big Cedar Mountain. Crab noticed that *the club had no choice but to put the trail up that mountain.*

Blood Mountain was immediately in front of us in all her majesty. For the size she is, *Crab realized that the trail up Blood was not as hard as it could have been.* To the far right, we even saw where we were going to be heading the next day.

In a single glance, we were looking at about two days of walking for an average hiker. *From our birds-*

eye view from beside the trail, we could see things that one could not see from an on-trail perspective.

As we headed down the mountain back towards the hostel, Mountain Crab began to have a different perspective about the grading of the trail. He said, "When the trail club could make the trail easy, they did. Other times the trail club had no choice but to take us over a difficult mountain. They even graded the trail the best they could." With his new perspective, he was thankful for the choices they made.

Branch took the analogy further. "Mountain Crab, the other day you were talking about God and evil. Just like our advantaged view today, God has a perspective that we don't have. The mountains represent our free choices. When God can be merciful, He is. However, He sometimes has to take us over the difficult mountains we have made for ourselves. God cares for us and graciously grades and routes the trail of life based on our choices."

Given his newfound perspective about the trail club's routing decisions, this explanation made sense to Crab.

Today's Scriptures: Psalm 33:13; Hebrews 4:13

Today's Action: Today I will live my life with the knowledge that nothing is hidden from God (Hebrews 4:13). If I follow His will, God will guide me down the paths of righteousness (2 Chronicles 16:9).

Today's Thoughts:

_____

_____

_____

_____

_____

_____

_____

_____

_____

Day 11
Short View Days

I have learned to be content with whatever I have. Fix your thoughts on what is true, and honorable, and right, and pure, and lovely, and admirable. Think about things that are excellent and worthy of praise. (Philippians 4:11a, 8b)

McAfee Knob in central Virginia is one of the most picturesque places on the entire Appalachian Trail. With feet dangling freely sitting atop this tabletop cliff, in one wide-angle view, hikers can drink in the mountains that they just completed and they can survey the mountains that they are walking towards. Peering downward, farmlands dot the Catawba valley like a green patchwork quilt. The green valley and the blue skies are a feast for the eyes.

For years we had looked forward to soaking up the scenery and snapping a prize photograph at McAfee Knob. The morning of the summit, we darted from the tent at first light to make good time.

After hours of hard hiking, we noticed that as we gained elevation, we were walking up into a cloud. Nervous about the clouded view at the pinnacle,

Branch bargained, "Maybe instead of a *feast* for the eyes, God will grant us a *snack* for the eyes."

As we rounded the final turn, thick fog began billowing all around us. As we foot-slogged to the summit, we hung our heads low when we saw the scenery. It looked as if someone had erased the surrounding countryside. Despite our best efforts, all we were served was cold, thick, soupy fog. Our emotions were clouded gray.

Sitting on the cold wet cliff, dumbfounded and defeated, we stared mindlessly into the fog. Just as all seemed like a loss for the day, a happy little bird landed near us and preached to us a sermon. Hearing that bird changed our perspective from being disappointed about missing a "vista-view day" to enjoying a "short-view day."

After the bird had finished his piece, with pep in our step, we began contrasting the gray fog with the brilliant spring colors. We also started smelling the sweet aroma of springtime accented by the tasty moisture in the air. Even the craggy rocks and the tree bark seemed to have more texture and interest.

As we hiked along, we beheld our surroundings with an excitement that we had not yet experienced. Around each bend, we felt like explorers discovering a completely new world awash with brilliant detail— detail that would have been disguised by the sun's glare. From this day forward, we were always excited about our short-view days.

Today's Scripture: Philippians 4:4-13

Today's Action: Despite the disappointment I'll face today, I will put into practice the perspective of Paul in Philippians 4. Seeing treasures at every turn, in every circumstance, I will learn to be content in Christ.

Today's Thoughts:

_____

_____

_____

_____

_____

_____

_____

Day 12
Keep Your Camp Holy

Designate a place outside the camp where you can go to relieve yourself. As part of your equipment have something to dig with, and when you relieve yourself, dig a hole and cover up your excrement. For the LORD your God moves about in your camp to protect you and to deliver your enemies to you. Your camp must be holy, so that he will not see among you anything indecent and turn away from you. (Deuteronomy 23:12-14)

A common joke with hikers is the question, "Where is the bathroom?" All too often the answer is that, in the woods, the bathroom is essentially every tree. This can present a problem.

Now, even in the woods, there is bathroom etiquette. According to Leave No Trace suggestions, we should bury waste at least six inches deep and a considerable distance from water sources, the trail, and camp. We have found that soft soil near a decaying tree is best. However, if you are hiking in the desert, then you should pack out your waste. This is because, in the desert, there is little water to break it down.

As silly or trivial as this may seem, rules about waste help us to get along with our neighbors. Every year on the various trails, there are stories about who laid their waste where and how it upset someone. For example, years ago, a field near a popular shelter in the Smokies was known for being somewhat of a dung-mine field. This is because there was no privy at the shelter. So, everyone did their business in the open field near the shelter—gross! Recently, a privy was built near the shelter and everyone is much happier.

Sometimes even the most seemingly-trivial rules have a greater purpose.

Today's Scriptures: Leviticus 11:44-45; 19:2; 20:7; 1 Peter 1:13-25

Today's Action: Today I will follow God's laws because they are good (I Timothy 1:8). By following God's laws, I will love God and my neighbor. I will keep my camp and life holy.

Today's Thoughts:

_____

_____

_____

_____

_____

_____

_____

_____

_____

_____

Day 13
Hike Naked Day

He (Moses) chose to share the oppression of God's people instead of enjoying the fleeting pleasures of sin. (Hebrews 11:25)

"Hike Naked Day" is a tradition on the trail during the first official day of summer—the Summer Solstice. Some long-distance hikers celebrate the day by hiking in the buff, going it naked, being completely without apparel! It is fairly common on this day to be startled by an encounter with a freedom-seeking hiker wearing absolutely nothing but his hiking boots and a backpack. Buck was a hiker who decided to "feel the freedom" of celebrating Hike Naked Day.

Buck was having a wonderful time hiking in the buff. The sun was shining brightly, there were plenty of trees around for coverage, and there was even a slight refreshing breeze. Buck made sure to avoid briers and bees in order to keep his birthday suit unblemished. As he strutted like a peacock down the trail, Buck's brimming confidence suddenly fell as the distinct sounds and smells of a crowded highway were just ahead. Knowing he would have to cross the highway to enter the woods again, hairs and goose bumps began to stand up and take notice all over his bare body.

A cold sweat came over him as he approached the bustling four-lane highway. He took a deep breath and peeked out of the forest, but the other side of the highway seemed miles away. So, to hide his shame, Buck reached for an impressive set of leaves that was close to him and he tucked them into the hip belt of his backpack. Now a little more veiled, he swallowed his apprehension, stepped out from the tree cover, and prepared to leapfrog through the speeding traffic.

Bobbing and weaving through the army of automobiles, he could feel thousands of eyes surveying his exposure. After what seemed to be an eternity, Buck scurried across the highway to the safety of the woods. Discarding the leaves, he laughed about the encounter now behind him, and continued celebrating the freedom of Hike Naked Day.

After crossing the highway, Buck's undefended exposure itched with increasing intensity. By the time he got to camp, raw red welts covered the unadorned area. He soon realized that he had grabbed poison oak to conceal his freedom! Reflecting on his mistake, Buck realized that freedom without restraint was costly.

Today's Scripture: Psalm 119:44-46

Today's Action: I am a slave to whatever masters me (2 Peter 2:19). Today I realize that my lawless "freedom" will be exposed (Numbers 32:23). However, I will rejoice because Jesus came to make me truly free (Luke 4:18-19). If Jesus has set me free, I am free indeed (John 8:36). So, I will follow God's laws (James 1:25; 2:12) and God's Spirit (2 Corinthians 3:17) because they provide real freedom. Neither will I use my freedom in Christ for evil (1 Peter 2:16) nor will I let my freedom in Christ be a stumbling block to my weak brothers (I Corinthians 8:9). Finally, when I do fall short, because of Christ's work, I will freely approach God the Father with humble confidence and ask for forgiveness and empowerment (Ephesians 3:12).

Today's Thoughts:

_____

_____

_____

_____

Day 14
Less On or More On?

As goods increase, so do those who consume them. And what benefit are they to the owner except to feast his eyes on them. (Ecclesiastes 5:11, NIV)

"Less On" was a lightweight backpacker. His pack weighed about twenty pounds. Because his pack was light, he was able to travel faster and farther on the trail.

"More On" was a heavyweight backpacker—very heavy weight. He only wanted to resupply once during his six-month thru-hike. Now, there is nothing wrong with extra gear but his pack weighed nearly one hundred pounds! It looked like a barge. While he had lots of top-notch gear, the weight of his pack caused him to hike very slowly.

Less On was willing to make do with less luxury and he did not mind improvising a little in order to carry less of a burden. He realized the inconvenience of having less was just for a season. Before putting an item in his pack, he asked himself whether it was a need or a want. Only necessary items made it in his pack. He also bought or made lighter equipment—a lighter backpack, a lighter sleeping bag, and a light tarp. Because he traveled light, he could get from town-to-town with greater ease and thus get more in-town rest. He eventually completed the trail.

More On was always thinking about scary "what if" scenarios on the trail. "What if it snows? What if I see a bear? What if I need more food? What if I twist my ankle?" His motto was "Travel light...freeze at night." His gear choices were motivated by fear. He bought a thick sleeping bag, a heavy hatchet, a big can of bear spray, a substantial knife, hefty hiking boots, lots of food, a big stove, and an abundance of fuel. While he slept and ate in luxury on the trail, because he traveled heavy, he was in the forest longer and he spent more time in town recovering. His knees were in constant pain. So, he had to get off of the trail earlier than he had intended. The trail was too taxing because of his burdensome backpack.

Back home, More On bought more great gear and was burdened by credit card debt because of it. The weight of his gear had damaged his knees on the trail and the doctor bill was high. He applied his "more is more" backpacking philosophy not only to his finances but to his faith. He burdened himself with every activity that the church offered and, because he was spread too thin, he was less effective.

Back home, Less On was frugal and lived within his financial means. He carried no credit card debt or consumer debt. He had a modest house and modest furnishings. He applied his "less is more" backpacking philosophy to both his finances and to his faith. Instead of burdening his time with superfluous religious activities, he focused on practicing and perfecting the basics of his faith. All else was chaff.

Now there is nothing wrong with carrying extra gear. *But your possessions should never own you.*

Today's Scripture: Galatians 5:1-3

Today's Action: Which person am I more like? Am I like Less On or am I like More On? Today I will begin the process of throwing off everything that spiritually hinders me (Hebrews 12:1) and I will no longer be financially burdened by lenders (Proverbs 21:20; 22:7; Romans 13:8). Jesus promises that He will help me though this process (Matthew 11:28-30; John 8:32).

Today's Thoughts:

Day 15
Bear Scare!

David said, "I've been a shepherd, tending sheep for my father. Whenever a lion or a bear came and took a lamb from the flock, I'd go after it, knock it down, and rescue the lamb. (1 Samuel 17:34-35a, The Message)

Clay led the way up the trail with Branch just a few paces behind. Enjoying the Green Mountains of Vermont, we snacked all day as Branch picked from the blackberry bushes lining the trail. The entire world was at peace to us. Our packs were light with little food because we were heading into town later that day. Our mood was further brightened by the knowledge that we would soon be sitting at a restaurant eating massive amounts of real, cooked food. Little did we know that a large animal would soon change our day.

As we neared the crest of a steep, rocky hill, Clay jerked to a stop so suddenly that Branch bumped into the back of his pack. With his eyes growing wider by the second, Clay focused on the chest-high brush to the front and left of us. The thick brush about thirty feet ahead began to move and part. A large animal was in there! Usually this was not a problem. Every animal we had ever encountered in the past had run away from us—from bear to moose—but not this one.

Clay was caught between fight and flight. With his heart pounding and with eyes like saucers, Clay clenched his jaw and shouted an urgent whisper back to Branch, "I think it's a bear!"

Hearing Clay's whisper, the line of shaking brush began rushing toward us. Clay barked, "Branch, get back!" Instinctively shoving Branch out of harm's way, Clay yelled to the beast, "Get out of here! Go!" Unphased, the moving brush continued to dash our way.

Tensing his grip, Clay raised his hiking pole, hoping to make the first assault. Catching a glimpse of its black fur in the brush, Clay braced for the fight. "You will not hurt my wife!" he shouted. At that moment the beast lunged out of the brush at Clay but, oddly, Clay lowered his pole.

Instead of the anticipated ferocious bear, it was a cheerful, medium-sized dog wanting to visit us! Unaware of the stress that he had just caused, the dog unabashedly licked Clay's outstretched hand as we began to breathe again. It seemed that today God was testing our character more than our strength (1 Chronicles 29:17a).

Today's Scripture: I Samuel 17:31-58

Today's Action: Like heroism, *character* is a quality you don't know whether you have until the moment of trial. Since character is like a muscle, today I will start a character building regimen for the day of testing (Psalm 7.8; Job 2:3, 9). My character is constantly on display and I will be a good example to others (Titus 2:7).

Today's Thoughts:

_____

_____

_____

_____

_____

_____

Day 16
Two Cents Worth

A gentle answer deflects anger, but harsh words make tempers flare. (Proverbs 15:1)

"Two Cents Worth" was the kind of woman you could hear long before you saw her. Her name fit her perfectly. Talking before thinking, she always made sure to put her "two-cents worth" into every single conversation. She had an opinion about everything.

Unfortunately, one night Branch became the target of Two Cents Worth's loose tongue. Two Cents had said something very hurtful and her words sat in the crowded shelter like a big fat elephant. It made everyone uncomfortable.

In the "everyday" world it is at this point that most people would begin digging through their imaginary bag of "social masks." Perhaps someone would choose to put on a nonchalant, happy face and maybe giggle a little. Or possibly, in order to hide the hurt, another person would choose an angry face and yell at the careless woman.

Branch prayed silently. "Lord please don't let me cry. Use this embarrassing situation for Your glory.

Keep me from sin. Give me wisdom." As she prayed, compassion for Two Cents Worth washed over Branch like a cleansing rain.

Branch realized that realness of character would get through to Two Cents Worth. So she swallowed hard and with a caring smile, Branch said, "You know what, Two Cents? It's okay. We'll both just move on."

Two Cents began to murmur an apology but Branch just assured her once again that they were going to be okay. Eventually the big elephant left the shelter and everyone was at ease.

The next day, Two Cents Worth caught up to us as we took a break on a mossy log on the side of the trail. She thanked Branch again for the way that she treated her. She even said that Branch showed true "grace" in the situation. Branch was jubilant.

Because of Branch's God-guided behavior, she was able to explain to Two Cents that her actions were not of her own strength but by the unmerited and borrowed strength of God. Now being comforted by the one she injured, Two Cents started having great spiritual conversations with Branch later up the trail. With social masks off, God was able to shine through Branch. His Word did not come back void! (Isaiah 55:11)

Today's Scriptures: Proverbs 15:1-3; 21:23;
James 1:26

Today's Action: When someone does me wrong
today, I will step back and see the real situation
through God's eyes. Instead of reacting from the flesh,
I will be God-guided and seek to minister to the
person through the power of the Holy Spirit.

Today's Thoughts:

_____

_____

_____

_____

_____

_____

_____

_____

_____

Day 17
Selfless Serving

Instead he lived a selfless, obedient life and then died a selfless, obedient death—and the worst kind of death at that—a crucifixion. (Philippians 2:5, The Message)

The trail is not a very sanitary place. Hikers sweat all day, sleep in dirty shelters populated with mice, and take showers once a week. To make things worse, hordes of hikers go into town to resupply and at least one person catches the latest sickness. That hiker then brings it back to the jam-packed shelters on the trail to share with the rest of the hiker population.

Unfortunately, Branch became victim of one such malady. It started with a tickle in her throat as we broke camp and it quickly spread to her entire body. By the end of the day, she was coughing uncontrollably and had fever, chills, and cold sweats. In the shelter that night, she kept everyone up as she tried to breathe through her congestion. By the next morning Branch was exhausted—along with everyone who had attempted to sleep in the shelter.

Since we were still in the wilderness, we had to make mileage or we would run out of supplies. We packed up, gearing up our minds for an all-day march. Clay took a good bit of the weight out of Branch's pack and was very encouraging, but he could not walk the fifteen miles for her. So, putting one foot in front of the other, Branch hacked, wheezed, shivered, and sweated with each turtle-sized step. During each short break, she nearly fell asleep. Finally, through the grace of God alone, Branch spotted the outline of the shelter. She had made it there!

When we got to camp, everyone who was already there ahead of us had heard of Branch's plight. They were even nice enough to help us find a location for our tent—making sure we were clearly out of earshot of the shelter.

Even though Branch was dog-tired, she did not expect a good night's sleep. Without medicine, all she could hope for was a night like the night before. As the veil of dusk surrounded camp, a young woman named Hippy Hopity came up to us as we prepared to enter our tent. She explained that she was getting over the same sickness and was truly concerned for Branch. Having boiled some water, Hippy Hopity offered some sleep-inducing cold medicine to Branch. Branch gratefully gulped down the medicine and drifted off to a deep, peaceful sleep.

The next day a hiker walked up to share our spot as we took a mid-morning break from hiking. He looked exhausted.

"What's wrong?" Clay asked.

"Man, no one could sleep in the shelter last night! Hippy Hopity ran out of medicine and kept everyone up with her wheezing!"

As Clay and the hiker continued to talk, Branch realized the extent Hippy Hopity's sacrifice. She had given up the last of her medicine, even going without it herself, so that Branch could find relief! Branch was overwhelmed by Hippy Hopity's selfless service.

Today's Scripture: Philippians 2:5-8

Today's Action: Today I will reflect on the sacrificial love that God has given me and I will strive to show that love to those He puts in my path.

Today's Thoughts:

_____

_____

_____

Day 18
Selfish Serving

Don't be selfish; don't try to impress others. Be humble, thinking of others as better than yourselves. Don't look out only for your own interests, but take the interest of others, too. (Philippians 2:3-4)

Innkeeper was ready to rest at the new double-decker shelter. He laid out his sleeping bag in a choice spot on the bottom floor and sat perched at the opening of the shelter. A few other hikers came in after him and everyone began settling in for the evening. Just as it was time to go to bed, a headlamp was seen bobbing in the distance coming towards the shelter.

Innkeeper was a famous hiker on the trail. Like many hikers, he loved to walk all day and sleep in the shelters. This, however, is not what made him famous. *Innkeeper was infamous for dictating who could sleep where in the various shelters on the trail.* That's why they called him, "Innkeeper."

As the head lamp came closer, we heard breathing. It was Lumberjack. Between wheezing breaths,

Lumberjack told us that he had hiked over twenty miles that day.

Like Innkeeper, Lumberjack was also famous. He too liked to hike all day and sleep in shelters. This is not what made him famous however. *Lumberjack was infamous for 'sawing logs' in his sleep. He snored...all night long.* That's how he got his name.

As Lumberjack surveyed the shelter for space, Innkeeper sprung into action. In a syrupy-sweet voice he intercepted Lumberjack as he began to drop his pack on the bottom floor of the shelter.

"No room downstairs in the shelter tonight, Lumberjack. No room. *Let me help you* get your pack upstairs." Appearing to be generous, Innkeeper shouldered Lumberjack's heavy backpack and started towards the ladder upstairs.

Yawning like a great cat, Lumberjack looked perturbed. "Man, I hate sleeping on the top floor! I am too tall to try to walk upstairs and it's such a pain to try to get up and down the ladder! But I guess I did get here late. Thanks for your help, Innkeeper."

Noticing Innkeeper's ulterior motive, Clay pointed to Innkeeper's sleeping bag and said, "Hey, wait! There is plenty of space right next to Innkeeper! Look, his gear is just spread out! You can sleep next to him, Lumberjack!"

With surprise in his eyes, Innkeeper looked at Clay with the intensity of a red laser. "No, no! The whole upstairs is open! Lumberjack will get a lot of rest up there! Besides, I plan to get up early and I don't want to wake him." Innkeeper shrieked as he tried to scurry upstairs with Lumberjack's pack in tow.

As soon as the words fell from the Innkeeper's lips, the shelter erupted with laughter. The motive of the Innkeeper was laid bare in this intense moment.

That night, Lumberjack slept well as his snore shook the entire shelter. Innkeeper, however, stayed up all night seething.

Today's Scripture: Philippians 2:3-4

Today's Action: As I serve others today, I will check my motives to make sure that I am not serving selfishly.

Today's Thoughts:

_____

_____

_____

Day 19
Fat Bladder

The Word became flesh and blood and moved into the neighborhood. We saw the glory with our own eyes, the one-of-a-kind glory, like Father, like Son, Generous inside and out, true from start to finish. (John 1:14, The Message)

Virginia Highway 606 is in the middle of nowhere. There is nothing really spectacular about it unless you are a hiker. During a hot May day we read in the guide that we could get ice cream at Trent's grocery at the road ahead. From the road it was only a ten-minute walk to get cool again.

Rip Winkle was a lively retired man from the United Kingdom. As we walked the trail, together we reasoned whether or not God could communicate with humans. We shelved the debate for a while to eat ice cream. Fresh from the trail, with his pack still on his back, Rip waited patiently in the air-conditioned line at the grocery store to pay for the ice cream. Looking around at the rustic setting, he was horrified as he noticed that a small pool of water had begun accumulating between his legs on the yellowed linoleum floor. It was starting to puddle and people were stepping in it.

In a shocked reaction to what he saw, he exclaimed loudly in his thick English accent, "Oh my bladder, it's leaking!"

What he meant was that drinking water was leaking out of his *hydration bladder*—a piece of gear made out of watertight plastic that is intended to hold liquid. It's a type of water bottle. The water from this bladder was leaking in his backpack, running down his leg, and pooling on the floor. Unfortunately, something was lost in the translation. What everyone heard in the country store was that this poor hiker's *urinary bladder* was leaking!

For a long, awkward moment, the silence in the store was deafening. He desperately sought to remedy the situation. So, he exclaimed in the same loud tone as to explain to the store, "No, no, it's just water on the floor!" This did not really help the already awkward situation, however.

From behind the counter, the cashier with the lazy smile said with a thick southern-drawl, "*Yeah, its "water" alright! I'll get a mop.*"

Despite being a little cooler from the ice cream, Rip was red-faced with embarrassment. Walking back to the trail, Rip smiled and said, "I guess only hikers understand hikers! He didn't understand me and I barely understood him."

Branch replied, "That's what we had been saying back on the trail, Rip. God can communicate in a myriad of ways. If God wanted to communicate with an ant, he could become an ant. But instead, He wanted to communicate with humans. So, He became a human." And with that, we continued our friendly discussion.

Today's Scripture: John 1:1-14

Today's Action: Today I will thank God for coming to communicate with us (Matthew 1:23). I will communicate with others to let them know that God wants to talk with them.

Today's Thoughts:

_____

_____

_____

_____

Day 20
Christianese

It's the same for you. If you speak in words they don't understand, how will they know what you are saying? You might as well be speaking into empty space. There are many different languages in the world, and every language has meaning. But if I don't understand a language, I will be a foreigner to someone who speaks it, and the one who speaks it will be a foreigner to me. (I Corinthians 14:9-11)

Evan was a good church-going man that was eager to evangelize. Grateful Ed was a hiker on the trail eager to learn about Jesus. Sitting together at a church dinner for hikers, they tried to converse.

With an awkward smile, Evan began by asking Grateful Ed his favorite question, "What has been the best time you've had on the trail thus far?"

With a gleam in his eye, Grateful Ed chuckled, "Ha! The other day I was in the zombie zone pink blazing NOBO through a puddy relo. I ran into some tourons who found my stealth. I yogied some mountain money and some magic from them. Then I scored an AYCE at the NOC. That ruled!"

Then Grateful Ed asked a similar question, "What do you all do here at the church?"

Still deciphering what was just said by Ed, excited Evan answered, "I am an ordained deacon and I lead the Adult 4 Nehemiah class. We used to just fellowship but we've 'repented' and now we're learning doctrine. In fact, last week I taught about transubstantiation, consubstantiation, and the sacraments. We are so blessed. Hey! You should come to our crusade tonight! Have you taken communion from church before?"

Startled, Grateful Ed said, "Man, I haven't taken *anything* from *any* church! I'm just here for dinner."

Ed smiled at Evan and Evan smiled at Ed and they began eating their dinner again without a word. Eventually, Ed found himself talking to the other church member at the table and Evan found himself talking to other hikers at the table.

Today's Scripture: Acts 17:16-34

Today's Action: It is amazing how many languages, dialects, colloquialisms, and accents are here on Earth. When speaking to the Greeks about God in Acts 17, the Apostle Paul made sure that he spoke in terms that the Greeks understood. He even used their own poets and statues to connect with them. Like Paul in

Acts 17, I will be sensitive to my use of Christian lingo in front of my non-believing friends so that I will communicate well today.

Today's Thoughts:

_____

_____

_____

_____

_____

_____

_____

_____

_____

_____

Day 21
Chiggers

Guard your heart above all else, for it determines the course of your life. (Proverbs 4:23)

Two Cents Worth was known for always putting in her "two cents worth" about everything. She had an opinion about all matters and she was not shy to share it. If anyone disagreed with her, she would often sling a sarcastic response or hurl a personal cut down at the person. That is the way she "won" the argument. If you expressed that your feelings were hurt from her personal attacks, her stock response was to advise you to just "get thicker skin."

Maybe she was right. Clay had always been told to have thicker skin—to let the comments roll off like water on a duck's back. Examining himself, he assessed that she might be correct.

Hiking together in central Virginia, we all stopped at a mountainside field to camp for the night. With a few hours left of daylight, the heat of the day still lingered.

Sitting in the grassy field with the other hikers, Two Cents exclaimed in passing, "Clay, why are you still wearing your long gaiters with your shorts on? Aren't you hot? You look silly. We aren't hiking right now!"

Now, you may not know what gaiters are. Gaiters are thick, cloth leg-coverings that start midway up a hiker's boot and cover up a portion of the hiker's leg. Clay was in the habit of wearing his gaiters often.

Probably being a little Pollyanna, he put on the thick skin that Two Cents suggested but he kept a soft heart and pondered what she had said. He thought to himself, "I love my gaiters. They keep my legs clean; they keep my legs dry; they keep my legs from being beaten up; and they keep bugs off me. I really love my gaiters!" So, he kept on wearing them.

The next morning he woke up invigorated. He had a great night's sleep. The grassy field had provided extra padding under the tent like a primitive mattress. Two Cents, on the other hand, had a terrible night's sleep.

Looking a little like a kangaroo, Two Cents hopped around the camp on one leg while furiously scratching. Branch asked her what was wrong and she revealed dozens of red welts on her ankles. She had been bitten by chiggers last night while sitting by the campfire!

Chiggers are pinhead-sized insects that feel like they are living under your skin. They seek out thin skin on mammals as their point of attack. Their bites can itch for days.

The pain of the bites softened the heart of Two Cents and she pulled Clay aside. "I wanted to apologize for what I said last night about the gaiters. I see that they protected you from the chiggers."

"That's okay" he replied. "It seems that both of us needed thicker skin while keeping a soft heart."

Today's Scripture: Proverbs 4:23

Today's Action: Words can be like chiggers. Sometimes words feel like they get under your skin. Today, I will be like a Leviathan (Job 41). I will have a thick skin and have a soft heart (Proverbs 4.23). If I am insulted, I will not be quick tempered (Proverbs 12:16). I will accept correction (Proverbs 5:12; 12:1). When wronged, I will be patient in bearing with my brothers and sisters (Ephesians 4.2). I will also be diligent to speak a good word to those around me (Ephesians 5:19).

Today's Thoughts:

_____

_____

_____

_____

_____

_____

_____

_____

_____

_____

_____

_____

Day 22
Burdens

Give your burdens to the LORD, and he will take care of you. He will not permit the godly to slip and fall. (Psalm 55:22)

We had planned to hike eighteen miles but, as it often happens, God had other plans. Hiking through the Grayson Highlands, winter waged war against spring. The result of their clash was an incredible display of weather's extremes. One minute we were bathing in the sunshine felicitously feeding the feral ponies, the next we were scurrying for cover from nickel-sized hail and torrential rain. By the time we made it to Old Orchard Shelter, the clash of the seasons had taken its toll. We were exhausted and weren't about to leave. The weather was just too bad.

"You're Branch aren't you! Hi! I'm Steppin' Wolf." a cheerful older lady called out as we laid out our gear in the shelter. "I heard you are a Christian. I just wanted to let you know that I am using this hike as my own spiritual journey."

By the time Branch picked her jaw up off the ground from the shock of such an incredible introduction, the moment to respond had passed.

Steppin' Wolf had begun talking with another hiker in the shelter but Branch prayed silently for another opportunity to talk.

As the sun dipped behind the mountains, the temperature dropped, and there was a mad dash for our sleeping bags. As God would have it, Steppin' Wolf's bag was right next to Branch's. Shivering in the shelter, it wasn't long before Steppin' Wolf began to explain the reason for her hike and her spiritual journey.

Steppin' Wolf was a Christian who had not felt near to the Lord for many years. Her life's story was as knotty as the old trees that had survived years of extreme weather on the alien-like terrain of the Highlands.

Hearing the heartbreak, Branch silently cried out to God, "Lord, I'm young and have little experience to offer this hurting sister." God reminded Branch that He is the Comforter (John 14:26), Counselor (Isaiah 9:6) and Healer (Exodus 15:26). Placing her hand on Steppin' Wolf's hand, Branch entreated her to cast her cares upon the Lord (Psalm 55:22). They prayed together and talked about living moment-by-moment directed and empowered by the Holy Spirit (Ephesians 5:18). By the time the last light of the day was snuffed out, Steppin' Wolf was sleeping more soundly than she had in weeks.

The next day, Steppin' Wolf thanked God and she thanked Branch. Trotting down the trail, she noticed that though her backpack weighed the same, it felt lighter as she had given her heavy burdens to the Lord.

Today's Scriptures: Matthew 11:28-30

Today's Action: Today I will give my burdens to the Lord (Psalm 55:22) and I will help to carry the burdens of others (Galatians 6:1-2).

Today's Thoughts:

_____

_____

_____

_____

_____

_____

Day 23
Rest

You have six days each week for your ordinary work, but on the seventh day you must stop working, even during the seasons of plowing and harvest. (Exodus 34:21)

Long-distance hiking is best described as perpetual motion and perpetual fatigue. After hundreds of miles of hiking, nearly everyone's feet go numb. Clay's foot grew a size and a half! It can take months for the swelling to go down after millions of steps. The motto on the trail is "No rain, no pain, no Maine!" That is, you have to go through a lot of rain and pain to make it to Maine. The human body starts breaking down and begging for rest. When this happens, it is good to take a Sabbath from your stress.

Examining the map, Clay made a happy discovery. We had already hiked ten miles before noon and had made it to the shelter—a "ten-by-twelve" in hiker lingo. No one really wanted to quit by noon, but the next shelter was fourteen miles away. In between the two shelters, the news was grim.

The guidebooks said that there was no water and no camping until the next shelter. This is because of a little obstacle in the way called Dragon's Tooth. Dragon's Tooth should be called "Dragon's *Jaw*" because it's a few miles of cliffs and craggy rock that resemble a narrow jawline. No wonder there was no camping or water.

As Clay looked at the map, Branch listened to the weather report on her radio. There was a seventy percent chance of thunderstorms in the afternoon for the area. "I guess Dragon's Tooth will have water today after all—straight from the sky," she said. This was enough to seal the deal for us. Thunderstorms and exposed ridgeline don't mix!

Filled with testosterone, our hiking companions wanted to keep hiking despite the danger and long mileage. Although we were having purposeful conversations, we needed a Sabbath. So, knowing we would meet up soon, we parted ways. We set up our tent and they began the long day on Dragon's Tooth.

Soon, the smell of moisture in the cool breeze began to blow through the tent. The rains had arrived. Concerned, we prayed for our friends' safety because we knew they were struggling through the storm. As for us, we were snug as bugs in our summer sleeping bags. Praising God for His wise commandment to rest, Psalm 46:10 set the theme for the remainder of the day, "Be still and know that I am God..."

Today's Scripture: Exodus 20:8-11

Today's Action: Today I will choose a day to take a Sabbath rest from my stressful living. I will choose to completely rest (Matthew 11:28), read God's word (Deuteronomy 17:19), and relax (Psalm 116:7).

Today's Thoughts:

_____

_____

_____

_____

_____

_____

_____

_____

Day 24
Free Meal

Then we will no longer be immature like children. We won't be tossed and blown about by every wind of new teaching. We will not be influenced when people try to trick us with lies so clever they sound like the truth. (Ephesians 4:14)

The Grayson Highlands in Virginia is known for its long-maned feral ponies that eat apples right out of your hand. Having trotted through the Highlands, we were as hungry as horses. So, we headed to the hostel at Troutdale Baptist Church for a shower and then to the Ma-and-Pa restaurant down the road.

We galloped to get food and we found ourselves to be first in line. As the six of us in our group sat around the table recounting the day, a somewhat tousled townsperson rolled in to the restaurant. As soon as he saw us, he raised an eyebrow and assertively approached.

With his lip curled he said in a drawl loud enough that the whole restaurant could hear him, "Y'all is thru-hikin' ain't ya? I hiked a lot of the trail myself— from South Carolina to here. Y'all represent American freedom! You're like American heroes to me! I'd like to buy y'alls dinner."

Without a word, Clay surveyed everyone's face at the table. "South Carolina isn't even part of the Appalachian Trail!" their furrowed brows were telling him. So, with a healthy dose of skepticism, he looked him in the eye, thanked him for the compliments, and politely rejected his offer on behalf of our group.

The man continued to compliment us, the trail, and America, and he was persistent in insisting that he pick up our tab. Over the course of just a few minutes of feeding our egos, some of our friends were hanging on his every word. Like a pied piper, he made it sound like we were doing *him* a favor by letting him pay for our meal.

As we all finished our free meal, the waitress came over and handed us our respective bills. Wide-eyed and grinning, the youngest member of our party puffed out his chest slightly as to correct the waitress. "Ours is paid for. The nice guy that was just in here said he's paying for our meal. I saw him tell you."

The compassionate waitress then told us the news. Apparently we had been conned by the town drunk! We should have used horse sense. As we paid our bill, the so-called "free meal" left a bad taste in our mouths the remainder of the night.

Today's Scripture: Proverbs 14:8; Jeremiah 17:9

Today's Action: Today I will be cautious of flattering words (Proverbs 26:28), I will be wary of a winking eye (Proverbs 16:30), I will test all things according to God's Word, and hold on to what is good (1 Thessalonians 5:21).

Today's Thoughts:

_____

_____

_____

_____

_____

_____

_____

_____

Day 25
Thunder Chicken

Goliath walked out toward David with his shield bearer ahead of him, sneering in contempt at this ruddy-faced boy....David replied to the Philistine, "You come to me with sword, spear, and javelin, but I come to you in the name of the LORD of Heaven's Armies—the God of the armies of Israel, whom you have defied. Today the LORD will conquer you..."
(1 Samuel 17:41, 45-46a)

It was time for a town day and our steps lengthened in anticipation of the meal and shower ahead. As we walked, we were immersed in deep conversation.

Having just listened to a riveting debate on our MP3 player, Clay said, "I loved how William Lane Craig used logic to point out the errors in his opponent's argument."

Branch replied, "Yeah. He would have definitely won in a scored debate, but I'm concerned that it was...."

"What's that?" Clay interrupted.

We stopped and listened. "I don't hear anything but a bird in some bushes." Branch replied as she pushed off of her hiking pole, resuming her town pace. "Anyway I think that..."

Then, all of the sudden...BAAM! Branch sprung backwards and yelled! Her pack slammed into Clay sending him sailing backwards into the ground. Loud, ear-piercing squawks mingled with Branch's screams. Clay could not see what was causing the commotion, but jumped to his feet in preparation to defend his wife. Branch continued to jump backwards and off the trail to get away. That was when Clay first saw the creature. Not knowing exactly what to do, he backed away along with Branch.

It was a huge chicken-like animal—too small to be a turkey and too big to be a chicken. Instead of being scared of us, it was angry, ready to charge, and even seemed ready to take us down. After a few moments of raucous squawking and charges towards us, the animal ran off into the bushes. So as not to further anger it, we made a huge circle around it as we passed by. We had survived seeing snakes, bears, and even moose before, but had never been so scared as by this encounter with the crazy chicken.

A couple of hours later, we ran into the ridge runner for the section. Ridge runners are hikers paid by trail clubs for on-trail public relations and to teach about Leave No Trace principles. Branch told him about the crazy chicken.

"Oh, that was a grouse!" he said laughing. "They cause people more fear than anything else. She probably had a nest in the bushes next to the trail and was making you pay attention to her to keep you away from her eggs."

This grouse had almost caused us to have a heart attack! What an impact such a small, basically defenseless animal had! She knew that it was her job was to protect her young. She was fearless to carry out that task, even when it meant to attack two huge "Goliaths" like us in order to accomplish it.

Today's Scripture: 1 Samuel 17

Today's Action: Like David, today I will trust in the Lord to conquer the giants in my life. I will not be afraid because I know that He is stronger than any foe.

Today's Thoughts:

_____

_____

_____

_____

_____

_____

_____

_____

_____

_____

_____

Day 26
Bad Map

Thy word is a lamp unto my feet, and a light unto my path (Psalm 119:105, KJV)

Our trail map said we only had about three miles left to get to the shelter. The map had laid out a pleasant future. With only ninety minutes remaining in our hiking day, we relaxed our step and daydreamed about the big dinner we would have later.

Two hours later, there was no sign of the shelter. "Maybe we walked a little too slow?" we reasoned. So, we kept hiking.

Two and a half hours later, our emotions were becoming clouded. Pooling our cartographic skills, we were sure we should have been there. So, we kept hiking.

Three hours later, the reassuring warmth of the sun was dipping behind the mountain. We were running short on water, low on patience, but abundant with stress. As the sun went down, so did our hopes, but we kept hiking.

Three and a half hours later, darkness cloaked its cold hand around us. Instead of hanging out with happy hikers huddled around a hot campfire, we heard the cold wind howl danger. So, we stopped hiking.

Making a quick campsite in a grove of thorns, we felt like prisoners surrounded by razor wire. With no water for cooking, we could not eat the meal we had dreamed about all day. With heads hung low, we chocked down few a dry morsels from our pack and crawled into our sleeping bags. "When did we miss the shelter?" was the question that raced through our thoughts all night. With cold wind crashing into our tent like ocean waves, we didn't sleep a wink.

The next morning, to our surprise, we were at the shelter within minutes. Our map had led us astray! At the shelter, signs were posted noting a *major relocation of the trail*. We needed a new map!

Without the right map, we misjudged how much farther we needed to walk, how much water we needed to save, and how fast we should hike. As a result our mental game was totally off. If we had the right map, our life would have been much easier.

Today's Scripture: Isaiah 41:23

Today's Action: There are many spiritual maps in the world. One test to find out whether these spiritual maps are correct is to determine how accurately they determine the future (Isaiah 41:23; Deuteronomy 18:17-22). Some say 'go this way,' others say 'here's a way,' but Jesus says that He is *the only way to God* (John 14:6) and over 300 predictions about him point to this fact. Today I will commit to the God of Israel, Elohim (Psalm 48:14), I will depend on the Holy Spirit to guide me moment-by-moment (John 16:13), and I will read the Bible closely as my spiritual map (Psalm 119:105).

Today's Thoughts:

_____

_____

_____

_____

_____

_____

_____

_____

Day 27
Walk Hundreds of Miles in My Shoes

Then Job spoke again: "I have heard all this before. What miserable comforters you are! Won't you ever stop blowing hot air? What makes you keep talking? I could say the same things if you were in my place." (Job 16:1-4a)

Hikers' personalities and backgrounds are as varied and colorful as the fall leaves. Retirees, military veterans, college students, and those in transition make up the majority of the varied hues of long-distance hikers. The trail brings people together from all seasons of life.

Making good mileage on a foggy winter day, we slowed our stride to greet a peculiar pipe-smoking hiker lounging on a log on the side of the trail. Wearing color-coordinated hiking gear, a splashy striped silk scarf, designer sunglasses, and a smile like a Cheshire cat, he looked more like an advertisement from a L.L. Bean catalog than he did a dirty hiker. His name was Artsy Al and he was from Australia. After a few minutes we gathered that Al worked in the modeling industry. This explained his seeming "fashion over function" philosophy about gear and clothing. After a few minutes of niceties, we said "goodbye" and he said "g'day" and we parted ways.

During the spring, we kept seeing Al at the shelters. He still dressed like a fashion plate and we still looked like hobos. Like the rhododendrons of the season, our friendship was starting to blossom as we continued to cross paths. Although we tented next to him each night and were close in proximity, we both recognized that we were worlds apart in our worldviews and lifestyles. However, despite the differences, we came to understand each other better the more we spent time together.

One night, taking a deep drag on his pipe, he expressed that he'd been hurt by church people previously. Folding his arms as we sat around the dying campfire, we sensed the church chat portion of the conversation had come to an abrupt end. Retiring to our tents, we realized that there were no words that we could say that would heal Al's hurt on this frigid night.

Day-by-day, we shared common struggles and celebrated successes. In time, we walked through everything together—the snowy winter, the rain and hail of spring, and the searing summer heat. By "walking a few hundred miles in his shoes," our friendship had seasoned.

One sunny day, instead of just meeting us at the shelter, Al raced to catch up to us. Out of breath, he asked us to talk with him. Our words and our works had weathered well under his scrutiny and, despite his previous hurt, God had allowed him to see Christ in us. Sitting in the middle of the trail over the course of a few hours, he began to ask question after question about the hope and joy we have in our lives.

Today's Scripture: Luke 24:13-34

Today's Action: Starting today I will practice what I preach (Psalm 50:16-17); I will be sensitive to and patient with those who have been hurt (Job 16:1-4); I will wait on the Holy Spirit's leading before I share my faith (Acts 16:6-7); and I will be willing to walk down the long trail of life with those different than me so that Jesus might reveal Himself in His time (Luke 24:13-34).

Today's Thoughts:

_____

_____

_____

Day 28
New Sight on the Road to Damascus

Then Jesus placed his hands on the man's eyes again, and his eyes were opened. His sight was completely restored, and he could see everything clearly. (Mark 8:25)

The Appalachian Trail is over 2,000 miles long but only about 3 feet wide. On a map, it appears as a line that parallels the east coast. From a birds-eye view it is easy to see how God often intersects this line.

While helping hikers in Georgia during thru-hiker season, we met a fellow with the trail name "Chicken Wing." Chicken Wing rolled into the gap after hiking about eight miles. It must have been a hard hike because he was wearing a scowl on his face. As he plopped down in one of our chairs, he lit his cigarette and began eating Little Debbie snack cakes we had offered him. We asked how his hike was going but the conversation was short. So, we tried to encourage him about his hike and we told him we'd see him in Damascus, Virginia at the Trail Days festival.

About a week or so later, we moved north with the harvest of hikers and began serving in North Carolina.

As we absorbed the serene setting of the mountaintop ranges surrounding us, a group of hikers joined us to drink in the view. We were surprised when a burly big-bearded hiker called Clay's name. It was Chicken Wing again! As we traveled down the trail together into the gap, we shared some food and swapped some stories. He was a little more trusting this time. As daylight escaped us, we wished him well and we reminded him that we would see him in Damascus.

About a month later we were in Tennessee. To our surprise, we saw Chicken Wing's hiking partner. His name was "Kentucky Fried." After sharing a Moon Pie with him and catching up about their hike, we bid our farewells, and we asked him to tell Chicken Wing we were thinking about him and praying for his hike.

By Damascus, Virginia, Chicken Wing sought us out at the church. He had an injury and we had volunteer doctors that could help him. After fixing his physical problem, a doctor also asked him about his spiritual ailments. With tears in his eyes, the man who was once calloused in Georgia, softened his heart and submitted to the Lord in Virginia.

Today's Scripture: Mark 8:22-26

Today's Action: Just as the blind man needed to be touched twice by Jesus in Mark 8, today I will be patient and realize that sometimes it takes multiple touches from the body of Christ to help the spiritually blind to see.

Today's Thoughts:

_____

_____

_____

_____

_____

_____

_____

_____

_____

_____

Day 29
Hidden Treasure

So we fix our eyes not on what is seen, but on what is unseen. For what is seen is temporary, but what is unseen is eternal. (2 Corinthians 4:18, NIV)

Hiking during a drought year, our water consumption had more than doubled during the summer. Running low on water on this arid section of trail, we put purpose in our pace after we read the guidebook to the trail. It revealed that the liquid treasure we longed for was at the next shelter—just a few miles away. Dust clouds rose up behind us as we hastened our pace. All we could think of was slaking our thirst.

Seeing the blue blaze on the tree ahead meant water was near. Putting a glide in our stride, we could not wait to sip from the cold mountain spring. At long last, we slid into the shelter, dropped our packs, and grabbed our filter and water bottles. Skipping past the sign that pointed the way to water, we finally made it to the spring...*but it was dry.*

"It's like the writer had either never been to this shelter or just assumed water would be here!" Branch barked to Clay. Hanging our heads low, we decided to take the safe route and push on another eight miles to get water at the next shelter. Our bodies and our emotions were dehydrated.

Slowing our steps on the way to the second shelter we met a local man with a long gray beard. He was picking wild mountain lettuce and ramps on the side of the trail. With passion and pride, he told us that his family used to own much of the land in this section of "the government trail." He asked us whether we wanted to see his land. "It is just off the trail." he coaxed. Even though we had "water on the brain" and wanted to make mileage, he assured us that his former home was just about one hundred yards down the hill.

We peered sheepishly into the dark woods and, even though we saw nothing, we followed him with hesitant steps. The woods seemed to close in on us. An American chestnut tree lay petrified on the ground as our feet began to find an old trail bed. Just as we were starting to feel a little petrified ourselves, the woods opened up into a small pastoral valley. Before us stood a big rustic barn, an old outhouse, and a gushing spring leading to a small pond. To our delight, our water woes were done for the day!

There was hidden treasure just off of the trail and we didn't even know it. We just needed the right guide to help us find it. Hiking along the rest of the day we thanked God for leading us to hidden treasures just off of the trail of life.

Today's Scriptures: Isaiah 58:11; Matthew 13:44; Revelation 7:17

Today's Action: Just as the majority of the resources are off of the trail, today I will ask God for guidance to find His Heavenly treasures.

Today's Thoughts:

_____

_____

_____

_____

_____

_____

Day 30
Blazes: White, Blue, Yellow, and Aqua

Don't look for shortcuts to God. The market is flooded with surefire, easygoing formulas for a successful life that can be practiced in your spare time. Don't fall for that stuff, even though crowds of people do. The way to life—to God!—is vigorous and requires total attention. (Matthew 7:13, The Message)

Buddha Dude had many goals in life. He had goals in business that his manager helped him to achieve, he had goals to lose his "corporate figure," and he had a goal to hike the entire Appalachian Trail after he retired. One day Buddha Dude's boss came into his cubical with tears in his eyes. Knowing his manager for many years and knowing that the economy was sour, it was obvious from his boss' expression that Buddha Dude's company was laying him off.

Since his business goals were blocked, he decided to pursue his alternative goals—hiking the entire trail and losing weight. Buddha Dude prepped to go to the trail with the intensity of a blushing bride preparing for her wedding. When the big day of the beginning of his thru-hike finally came, he took a deep breath of the foggy mountain air and touched the first *white blaze* on Springer Mountain. Clutching his hiking pole, it was as if he was on hiker holy-ground. Even though he knew the journey would be difficult, he was committed to experience every *white blaze* on the trail.

Cursing his corporate gut and his creaky bones, over the first few weeks he realized that hiking was even more difficult than he expected. Even though he was serious about seeing the trail, he found solace with the party crowd. The party crowd did not care so much about hiking past each blaze. "It's hip to skip" was their motto and "a smile per mile" was their goal. They just wanted to have a good time—and that was fine for them. They were hiking their own hike but this was not his hike. So, hanging out with his new friends, he started skipping parts of the trail. Besides, their parties helped to drown out the little voice inside that urged him to be true to his original goal and struggle past each *white blaze*.

The party crowd taught him the joy of *blue-blazing* (i.e. hiking alternative trails), the art of *yellow-blazing* (i.e. hitchhiking), and the thrill of *aqua-blazing* (i.e. floating down a river). Some hikers even *pink-blazed* (i.e. chased after women). This made the trail seem shorter, more fun, and certainly easier.

Near the half-way point, Buddha Dude was ready to quit. Nothing had really gone the way he had planned. Ready to order his plane ticket home, he picked up the phone to make the call and it rang in his hand. His jaw dropped when he heard the voice of his manager from the corporation on the other end of the line! He too had lost his job and he wanted to hike alongside Buddha Dude for the remainder of the trail! Buddha Dude danced around the room as his hope overflowed. He had newfound energy to hike again!

Meeting at Harper's Ferry, West Virginia, Buddha Dude and his manager embraced. The manager was surprised to find out that Buddha Dude had been skipping trail. This was not his original goal and he never took shortcuts at work. So, the manager reminded Buddha Dude that worthwhile goals have difficulties (James 1:2-4). United as a team again, they agreed to walk past every *white* blaze—no matter how difficult.

As tough as the northern states were, they pushed past the temptation to take shortcuts. Touching the sign on the last mountain together, Buddha Dude expressed thanks about the sense of accomplishment his manager had helped him to feel during the last half of the trail. He enjoyed the last half of the trail so much, he decided to hike the first half of the trail with the same sense of discipline. So, the manager suggested that they fly south and start back at Harpers Ferry walking south during the winter—walking past each *white blaze* of the first half of the trail—and they did...together.

Today's Scripture: James 1:2-4

Today's Action: Spiritual discipline is difficult. So, today I will crown Christ the King of my life, I will train myself to be godly (1 Timothy 4:7-8), I will press on toward my spiritual goals (Philippians 3:13-14), I will walk in a manner worthy of God (Ephesians 4:1; Colossians 1:10; 1 Thessalonians 1:12), I will stay on the narrow path (Matthew 7:13), and I will seek a godly mentor to help me achieve my spiritual goals (Proverbs 16:21-22).

Today's Thoughts:

_____

_____

_____

_____

About Appalachian Trail Servants

Rev. Craig and Suzy Miles are founders and directors of Appalachian Trail Servants, Inc.—a non-profit ministry. The purpose of their ministry is simple:

Connect to God, to hikers, and hikers to God
Conserve God's world
Serve God by serving hikers

Their vision is to send godly hikers to the trails of the world, build trailside "Hospitality Houses" (i.e. hostels, bunkhouses, summer camps), and host hiking conferences.

Over the years, the trail ministry in which they serve has been featured in over twenty-five print, radio, and television interviews.

For more information about the Miles' and the ministry in which they serve, visit www.trailministry.org.

All of nature seems to direct us towards God.
Even our hands can teach us how to know
God personally.

Hold out your hand
and read the next page
to begin your own
life-changing adventure with God.

How to Know God Personally

1. <u>Thumbs Up</u>: Great news! God *loves* you and has a *plan* for your life—John 3:16; 10:10

2. <u>Accusing Index Finger</u>: Bad news. *Everyone has sinned.* Sin separates you from God and His plan for your life—Romans 3:23; 6:23

3. <u>Center Finger Taller Than Other Fingers</u>: Jesus stands spiritually above everyone. He was *sinless* and He *rose bodily* from the dead. Because He is worthy, He is *able to bridge the gap* between you and God. Jesus provides the *only way* to experience God's love and plan— John 14:6; Romans 5:8; 1 Corinthians 15:3-6

4. <u>Wedding Ring Finger</u>: You cannot pay for your own sins. You must place *trust* in Jesus to pay for all of your sins and you must *commit* to Jesus to be King of your life—John 1:12; 3:1-8; Titus 3:5; Ephesians 2:8-9; Revelation 3:20

5. <u>Pinky Finger</u>: The pinky is the smallest finger. You must humbly receive Jesus on the throne of your heart. Bow your head now and humbly ask Jesus to pay for your sins and rule your life.

Made in the USA
Charleston, SC
17 January 2010